CANDLES BURN IN MEMORY TOWN

Poems from both sides of the wall

edited by Janine Pommy Vega

SEGUE

Special thanks to the New York State Council on the Arts for the funding that made this anthology possible. Thanks also to James E. Sullivan, Superintendent of Sing Sing Correctional Facility; Dennis Manwaring, Supervisor of Special Subjects in the Education Department, for their support of the writing program the last four years. And to James Sherry for his enthusiasm and expertise.

Production by Susan Bee
Typeset by Skeezo
Cover photo: Robert Matuszewski
Photo of Dickenson by Ira Cohen; All other photos by Angelo Jannuzzi

ISBN: 0-937804-29-0
Library of Congress Catalogue Card Number: 88-060340

SEGUE BOOKS
are published by
The Segue Foundation
303 E. 8th St.
New York, N.Y. 10009

Hector Algarín's poem, "To a Lifer, Who is a Friend of Mine," appeared in *The New York Times*, Sunday, January 26, 1986.

Some of Chuck Culhane's poems have appeared in *Bomb, Longhouse, Fortune News, Appearances, Choices, Central Park, Albatross, Cold Spring Journal, Witness,* and *Light from Another Country*. The poem "After Almost Twenty Years" won 2nd prize in the 1986 PEN Annual Award for Prisoners. The poem "Of Cold Places" won 1st prize in the 1987 PEN Annual Award for Prisoners.

George-Thérèse Dickenson's work is excerpted from a forthcoming book, *The Interpreter of Dreams*.

Some of James Douglas's poems were published in *Evergreen* and *Call It Me,* an anthology. He has read these poems over WBAI in New York.

Some of Henry Johnson's poems have appeared in: *The Light from Another Country, Viaztlan, Contact II, New York Quarterly, Green Feather: Poetpourri,* and *Blackbear*.

Some of Jackie Ruzas's poems have appeared in: *The Irish American Voice, Saiorge U-Eihrearin, The American Poetry Review.* Jackie also won first prize in the 1982 PEN awards for prisoners with his short story, "The Day the Kept Lost Their Keeper."

Janine Pommy Vega's poems have been published in *Exquisite Corpse, Alpha Beat Soup, Third Rail #7, Artist's Call,* and *Witness*.

Dedicated to Hector Algarín:
Whose poems, when he read,
were filled with duende.

CONTENTS

INTRODUCTION

This anthology is the result of a poetry workshop in Sing Sing Correctional Facility that has been going on, uninterrupted, for the last four years. That in itself is a minor miracle.

What began as a seed of an idea among Chuck Culhane, Hank Johnson, Jackie Ruzas, and James Douglas has grown into a long-term commitment to writing. Prison is not confined to inmates. It is a very definite part of our society, and there are two sides to every wall.

Somebody asked me once, in the middle of a prison workshop, what I was doing there. It was a fair question. I said I needed to work in situations where change was possible. Prison is one of those situations. Effecting change and being affected: a simultaneous process.

In the course of workshops at Sing Sing, there stopped being a "creative writing teacher." We became colleagues who shared the responsibility for bringing in new ideas, encouraging newcomers, critiquing each other's work. This anthology is the outcome of that interchange. Prison provided the place.

Hank Johnson said a great thing at the first Sing Sing Christmas Poetry Reading, in 1985. He said, "I'm a poet who happens to be in prison. Not the other way around." When we got down to selecting for the anthology, the regular members of the workshop insisted that George-Thérèse Dickenson and I be included not as editors but as poets, since we had written, and worked, and experienced the same intensity they had, week after week.

After long deliberation, George and I agreed. They were right. The workshops had touched and changed all of us. Both sides of the wall.

Janine Pommy Vega

HENRY JOHNSON

Henry Johnson was born in Brooklyn, and educated at Skid-more College and New York Theological Seminary. He has been a winner in the PEN Writing Awards for Prisoners and recipient of the Madeline Sadin Award. His poems have appeared in the *Greenfield Review Press, Contact II, The New York Quarterly, Poetry Society of America Bulletin,* and *Blueline.* He is looking for a publisher for his chapbook, *The Problem,* and is currently work-ing on his first book of poems. He lives in Ossining, New York. He teaches poetry workshops at Sing Sing Prison.

THE JOURNEY

Frantic, she hurries along the road.
It is moments before curfew,
Sirens rip the dusk like old rags.
There is laughter from the shadows,
No room for bird-songs.
The ruts in the road are deeper
Than Elsa's courage tonight. Missing
Stones as she runs, her child's voice
Whispers in her ear, and fear blooms
Crimson in her heart. The trip is long.

And there is nothing a soldier won't do
On a lonely road in Salvador.

Ossining, New York, 1986

THE BLUES SINGER

(for B.B. King)

When you stepped up
On the small stage

In the famous night club
Packed with people

Faintly glowing
From their expectations

A deep hush hovered in the air
Like smoke

In a mellow baritone
You tossed your songs

Out into the crowd
Like rose petals

Your feelings must have grown
Too hot for you to contain them

So you threw back your head
And began to croon

The blues so sweet
Your tongue melted

Forcing you to hum
The rest of the words

Ossining, New York, 1985

THE LEMPA RIVER

On March 18, 1981, an estimated 4,500 to 8,000 unarmed refugees — mostly women and children — tried to flee Cabanas Province. Their destination was neighboring Honduras, just across the Lempa River. Shortly after dawn their hopes of freedom turned to screams of despair as concealed Salvadoran army troops began peppering them with automatic-weapon fire and mortars.

—Hustler Magazine

my body is slick with blood, my banks
littered with the dead and dying, i have watched them
come by the thousands, weary campesinos, watched them flee
towards the folded arms of Honduras.

they always pretend to be unaware of the movement,
of the soldiers hidden cleverly in tall grass
if only I could close my eyes! shut out the cries
and hopeless pleas, the indifference of Honduran fishermen
who shake their heads and grumble
each time they must remove

the bodies of little children
from their fish traps.

SEARCH FOR LOVE

To search for love is futile in this den
Of sad, but deadly men, whose limp ardor
Drifts this prison sea, seeking warm harbors.
Yet we will do so again and again,
Probing each other with lopsided grins
Aimed at warding off these cold, cruel fetters
Of shame. When the warm voices of letters
Written long ago have grown chilled and thin,
Some of us might slit our wrists and throats
In our lonely prison cells. Death won't brake
Our search for human feelings in this boat
Of chaos. There's far too much at stake:
To live unloved makes us cold, cruel, remote.

Comstock, New York, 1984

BALLAD OF JUANITO PAZ

He was never without
His old transistor radio
Tied to his wrist
By a piece of ribbon
Pilfered from the marketplace
In San Vicente.

No one in his village knew how, or
Where the boy got them, but
He always had enough batteries
To hear the promises and threats
Piped daily through government radio.

No one in his village could resist
His impish smile
Nor remain angry at his habit
Of walking along winding, dusty roads, alone
A yellow radio pressed to his ear
Like some strange seashell.

There is no playground like Salvador
That world of chattering guns
Trees, walls, and stones stained with blood
No sanctuary from the terror of privilege
Or armies that come and go
Like summer storms in the mountains

And it makes no difference who dies
In the flood of war,
Or that a little yellow radio
Hangs from the belt
Of a killer.

Ossining, New York, 1986

14

TRANSCENDENCE

for John Coltrane

your smooth
chromatic
riff
rises
like angel's
breath

speaks
to us
in all
keys

moans
a message
we vaguely
recall

compels
your
fingers
to tell
a story

a love
story

too
beautiful
for words.

Ossining, New York, 1987

WALKING ALONG THE ROAD

a baby skunk, dried blood
spread around the terribly
flattened body

lies in the wind-swept road
near the guard rail.
At the edge of the road

the fringed gentian
are spreading their petals
festive, their pale violet

luminous in the daylight,
their long stems
deep green.

Ossining, New York, 1987

ELEGY FOR A MISSISSIPPI SLAVE

You were hoping you would faint,
or that the master would change
his mind and begin
untying the straps
binding your wrists;
but as your dream of mercy peaked,
a new bull whip
cut gashes bone deep
into your back.

You had never touched a girl
nor dared cast your eyes
upon the bloodless belles
imprisoned in rustling silk and ribbons;
and you could not have dreamed
of grabbing anyone
by the throat,
or pulling her
into a hay-strewn stall
like a field nigger.

You screamed once
while the master cursed you
and stole one scathing look
at Prudence
who mocked you
with her false eyes.

Ossining, New York, 1986

DREAM OF ESCAPE

The free side of the walls
Night, warmth, a parking lot.

But no keys.

You hear the sirens
shatter the fragile calm,

the yellow stench of fear,
thick and rolling in
like fog

filling every shadow.

The guards scurry out
in force
and they form a line,

their faces painted
beneath their swat caps,

brandishing imaginary guns
in the prison yard.

You decide to flee
through the dense woods,
where people line the trail

holding out cups of cold
vintage wine.

In front of you
a wood nymph

insinuates herself
between you and freedom,
promises pleasures

long denied.

You join her
for a few fierce seconds
of tenderness

in a clearing
hidden from all eyes

but the stars.

Ossining, New York, 1987

SONG FOR DR. MARTIN LUTHER KING JR.

This was the state of things.
Love propelled you into a history
Peopled by angry mobs lined up

In incredible gauntlets of hate.
You could have stopped then,
Turned back, forgotten

The whole frightening idea; but
You were made of sturdier stuff than that.
Neither bricks nor bats wielded

By the seed of a proud Confederacy
Were strong enough to halt your love.
Like Antaeus, each time you were flung

To the ground, you rose with renewed strength,
Took another torturous step toward the dream.
In time, the gauntlets dispersed like a river fog,

And the road stretched before you to the mountain top.

Ossining, New York, 1986

20

PRISONERS OF THE SIX O'CLOCK NEWS

they're at it again:
mobs of angry whites
in hot pursuit of blacks
who dash like foxes
from a pack of murderous dogs

unfortunately, not all blacks
run like Jesse Owens, so
the slow ones are left behind—
some escape, some don't

in the inner cities mothers
prisoners of the six o'clock news
are afraid of what they'll hear
of what they'll see

the anchor person
reports that a black youth
has been killed, but holds back
his identity for effect

and the mothers
lean forward in their seats
wringing their hands, glancing expectantly
at their apartment doors.

Ossining, New York, 1986

THE HUNTER

Though the grass is short, he presses himself
Flat to the earth like a half-buried stone,
Ears pulled tight against feline skull, eyes bright,
Now sneaking up like a burglar,
Or a cop on a crook, careful, careful,
Dashing forward when the gull turns its head,
Stops, rushes forward, and stops again,
Watches closely, becomes a fur statue,
Muscles taut and coiled like springs, moving slow,
Creeping, creeping, creeping—gotcha!

Ossining, New York, 1986

REVOLUTIONS

for Nat Turner

In a sermon you preach about the vision.
It is the sound of chains snapping in the woods,
like blues in some slave song in Virginia.
Like most revolutions, yours begins at home
bathed in the greenish blue color of the sun,
images of faces swollen purple, swaying
like strange fruit in the trees.
It is rumored that you are a runaway in Maryland,
caught, drowned. The hope of fools.

There is no escape from the anger of centuries,
or the congregation banging at your door.

Ossining, New York 1987

23

LOVE POEM

It no longer matters
How vast the desert

Our love has drifted into
Year after year after year

We should be thankful
For surviving love's drought

Thankful that our marriage
Was not discovered

Scattered like bleached bones
At the edge of boredom.

Ossining, New York, 1986

NO ONE ANSWERED

your door
so I let myself in

I gathered all your jewels
and silverware for safe-keeping

where no one
can find them

not even
you

THE ROOT WORKER

Everything you've heard is the gospel truth.
We were all there. His son wore a bone
in his nose. His wife sat smiling,
his daughter crept out of the house
when he wasn't looking. There were wood carvings
on the walls, human skulls, a spear standing
near his ratty armchair. The stars burned holes
in the night. James Brown screamed at us
from the cathedral radio. He was hoarse.
All of the windows in the house had bars on them.
We ate supper, roast pig, candied yams, cornbread,
a young girl stood silent near the table. The girl
brought dried fruit, raisin wine, some sweet potato pies.
We were offered something strange to smoke.
Drums began thumping from somewhere in the house.
His wife caught a fit. Spoke in tongues. His niece
fed the leftovers to something growling in a dark corner.
The subject of magic came up, stories of lost spells.
A dog began to howl out back. The root worker
mumbled something, stormed outside with a knife in his hand.
We wanted to leave, but were afraid. He returned
carrying a bloody sack used to bag grain.
He spilled a mess of eyes onto the floor. They gleamed
like fresh squid. We're telling you the truth.
He filled both hands with eyes, smeared them all over
his bony chest. The eyes looked at us then. It is
the only way, he swore. If you want a woman to love you
you have to be man enough to cry. He grabbed his beard
and cut it off with his knife. Every gesture has meaning,
he said. He was one-hundred-ten years old. A few of the eyes
on the floor watched us closely. A few of the eyes
on the floor saw the passion die in our hearts.

Ossining, New York, 1987

26

JACKIE RUZAS

My birthdate shows forty-four years, but I hover anywhere between the ages of fourteen and eighty-four. I have been one of the Kept for the past fourteen years, and I've known some joy, but more sadness in between. Any more bio would bore me, so to the reader I say, "Know me through my writing, and the friends I keep."

To Chuck, Hank, Jimmy, Hector, Janine, and George-Thérèse: you have all added something wonderful to my life.

WHERE OR WHEN

Huddled under a tent with strangers,
my woolen clothes soaking wet.
Sharks swim undisturbed over cars, grass,
and concrete dividers.

Hiding in a tree I watch Mom argue with
the seltzer man. He enters my yard. I climb
down from the tree into—a prison yard
where Frankie "Bones" and Georgie Bates
are playing gin with comic size Alice in Wonderland
cards. Their bodies petrified, clay like
resembling Homo Antiquitus in the Hamburg Museum.
I pass them by.

The yard becomes a winding road, desolate.
I walk and walk as seasons fall behind me and
voices fill the night.

Sing Sing, 1985

MAY 5, '81

The sun burns bright in the cloudless sky
warming the cell-block brick.
Through an open window comes a soft spring
breeze to chase away the prison stale and
dry my socks on the old string line.
I peer through the rain-stained windows and one
inch bars at the old maple tree in the yard,
soon to shade the chess player and jogger out
of steam. A sound, my eyes fall to the window
ledge. Mr. & Mrs. Pigeon, squatters through the
winter cold, now cuddle n' coo, new parents to
the little egg.
A friend's voice calls from eight cells away.
"Jackie, I just heard on the radio, Bobby Sands
died."
A long silence, our vigil over, the breeze is
still.
"Not dead Micko. Never dead, just free at last."

Auburn, 1981

MARGARET POWERS

She sees the soldier's boot
  smash through the tired door
an alien invader intruding on her seventy years.

In proud defiance she stands
  as have generations of mothers before
and smiles inside her heart at the sound
  of the back window, her son's escape.

Her swollen ankles and soft lined Irish face
  have appeared at many a prison gate
where she stands erect and demands
  no better treatment than—just let him be.

Margaret Powers has walked the mother's walk
  down tear-stained cobblestone streets
to protest her son's life under guard or
  underground.

Glory O, Glory O,
  to the soul of Margaret Powers,
Glory O, Glory O,
  to the bold fenian Ma.

Sing Sing, 1986

ODE TO A CORPORATE SLAVE

(Jackie to Loretta)

Better you cannot see yourself
through my eyes.
Cellulite laden, valium driven wimp
to a Corporate Khan
riding out the years on a
carousel of Con-End security,
while your heart yearns to
sell silk blouses in a Houston boutique.

Why do you resent my attitude?
Because I favor your dream
while you kowtow to your employer?
Because I prod you towards tomorrow,
while you grip tight reign on today?

A half century has passed
in a life not guaranteed.
Risk your dream.

Sing Sing, 1985

I COULD SCREAM

(Loretta to Jackie)

I cannot break my parts down
and self-assemble,
nor ride your marshmallow cloud of escape.

Life has given me responsibilities
that burden my dreams, yet measure my worth.
I am a woman more comfortable in a negligee
than a business suit, but I am not a whore,
and business suits pay my bills.

Yes I am a coward, but if you fail
to understand my weakness,
I will have wasted twelve years loving you.

Sing Sing, 1985

LISTEN, PLEASE

Perhaps your greatest sin
is the resentment that sours my soul.
Razor sharp lies score my mind
in rapier movement.

You have trampled the
garden I welcome few to water.
Precious flowers that decorate
a friend's existence wane colorless.

From a distance I watch you
stumble confused, gnarled fingers grip
the next feeble excuse. How blind can a
seeing person be? How bewildered?

I see more than you know,
understand it all, agree to little.
Take my hand before you lose it.
Take my hand before the gardens freeze.

Sing Sing, 1984

MR. PLANT

Observe the slow gait on
legs long denied full sprint,
yet his pace is steady and
the concrete beneath, impressed

Shadows in the night add lines to his face
the bard with blue eyes
The brother, son, and holy being
whose religion knows no church

A challenge echoes like some beastly roar,
his sword a little empty belly
goes forth to meet the injustice
the food of conviction his armor and ally

In time to come a stranger's hand
will carve his journey on quarried stone,
and I'll plant a daisy or push one up
at the toll of the bell.

Sing Sing, 1986

EASY TO KILL

The door.
I can see its molding if I scrunch in the
    left corner of my cell
    and peer through the bars to my right.
Each morning I awake
    one day closer to death.

The prison priest, a sometime visitor,
    his manner warm, asks,
    "How are you today? Anything I can do for you, son?"
"Is it just that I'm so easy to kill, Father?"
    His face a blank, he walks away.

Play my life back on this death cell wall,
    I wish to see my first wrong step.
To those who want to take my life,
    show me where I first started to lose it.

Madison County, 1975

STEPS IN TIME

His shackled legs took one step at a time
down the staircase he had walked all the
seasons since his birth

Nowhere was his destination.
No sanctuary was his lot.
No pillowed breast softened his aloneness.

He felt the shove, and knew the gnarled
fingers of the gargoyle at his back
celebrating each tortured step.

The steel rubbed raw against the bones
of his ankles, and he offered up the pain
to all the legless of Vietnam.

He saw signs of light and felt the
rush of a rebel prepare him for his
final step.

It came, he took it, then turned
and did a light soft shoe.
In the face of the gargoyle, he danced.

Attica, 1987

36

THE BUS RIDE

The bus travels the Thruway from past to future,
I sit by a window somewhere in between.
Another trip, another transfer, another prison
at day's end.

It is summer and a lush green landscape spreads
out from the Thruway to mountains that touch the sky.
I didn't know I loved the color green.
Green, the color of life, so hard to be in winter,
praises summer for its chance to be.
She had green eyes and black hair. I had green eyes
and black hair. She wore my ankle bracelet.
I wore her name, Camille, on my garrison belt.
We shared an eclair on a bench in Linden Park.
She took a bite. I took a bite. We kissed in the
middle, so long ago.

The billboard shows a Budweiser face, "Milwaukee's
Favorite Beer."
I didn't know I loved beer.
An eleven year abstinence from the me who helped
construct the Big Apple from scaffolds in the sky.
My throat recalls the taste of malt and barley.
Two adolescent fingers held up outside the Tumble Inn
Bar meant two quart containers. A climb over the back
fence, a dollar passed through the window to old Tony's
feeble fingers, the sale made. An hour later the fence
was a trap that brought six stitches.

A rabbit! Was it a rabbit I saw scamper through the
woods?
I didn't know I loved rabbits.
His name was Bugs, and I got him from Ol' Farmer Steve
who now presses grapes to wine in heaven.

My uncle didn't want rabbit shit in the cellar,
so Bugs froze to death in the battered doghouse,
while I slept snug in my child's cocoon.

I didn't know I loved bus rides.

Attica/Sing Sing, 1983

BLUE AND YELLOW FLOWERS

(Dedicated to Barbara)

"I love you,"
I whispered to the cell wall
its paint peeled surface
a jagged pattern surrounding
the pencil drawn hearts.
The wall is beige, the hearts are charcoal,
our love is blue and yellow flowers.

Napanoch, 8-23-87

JAMES DOUGLAS

James Douglas was born somewhere in America. He graduated from Marist College, and received his master's degree from New York Theological Seminary. Some of his poems were published in *Evergreen Magazine*, and *Call It Me*, an anthology. His work has appeared in the *New York Times*, *Jet*, and *Ebony*. He has read his work over WBAI. For the last nine years he has worked for Literacy Volunteers of America.

HOPE

I am hermetically sealed
in concrete and steel
but I have hope

On weekends and holidays
I sit in the yard and look
through metal wrapped cracks
at the Hudson River

Ah! the beauty
to watch multicolored sails
glide up and down
the polluted waters

Hope and fantasies are born
cultivated hate is stilled and
the pursuit of death is waylaid
a little while...
then I can think about Betty

May 1986

WISHFUL THINKING

She has waited so long for me
year after year after year.
My better half is a cut diamond,
pure as a January thaw.
I know what she is doing tonight,
Friday night...she is sitting at
home curled up in her favorite
corner of our old couch. She has
just finished bathing and oiling
her body. Now she sits thinking
of me. I can see her, rolled up
in her corner dressed in her
Teddy Bear shoes and purple robe.
I smell her body under the musk
oil, it overwhelms me. Yes, I
see her, she is disrobing for me.
As if in a trance, she removes her
robe. Her breasts are sagging
from time and overuse, but there
remains a timeless beauty in them.
She has grown round, her waist
and buttocks are no longer firm.
Yet her body glitters like a black
diamond. The pastel light from
the table lamp glides over her
dimensions, and I smile.
She is waiting for me.

March 1987

THE HUNT

I will kill a bear or a wild boar
Into the woods I went
At the edge where I entered
The sun peeped in
As if on a spying mission
I walked, became drunk
With a passion to kill
Moss covered the trees above
The sun abandoned its work
With my twelve gauge
It was the natives and I
Wild boars and black bears
With hunting skills
I stepped into an Olympic arena
Where bleached bones told the
Story of many a war fought
And the bones looked as if
They had never been the frames
Of meat and muscle
Fight or flight looking in the
Eyes of a razorback boar with
Tusks as long as my index finger
The hunt ended without a single shot
The race was on
Victory in the sun

LOOKING BACK

The windows of my mind reflecting
on the past

Washing funky clothes and dreaming
of owning a washing machine

Cooking black-eye peas, rice, pig's feet,
and a rhythmic sound coming from the washboard

Lawd hab mercy, I so tired...
I so tired, and my feet hurt so bad

...Jimmy cut som wood and
bring hit in de kitchen

Shit boy! Do u wanna eat?
U don't hab to be a nigga cause folk says so

U gone git dat wood fo u dada come home
and u know he don't be wonting no shit

Lula Mae u be keeping u legs
shut fo u git koched

Dat what dat gal ub miz Alice Mae say
and lookit dat belly

Gal u don't talk back at u mama...
U don't hab de say it, u eyes done doneit

Lawd lookit dat boy u lil
nocked nees cockeyed fool

U know u ony hab two ob doz britches
and u on u nees, git u ass offen u nees

U o' hickory head boy u nebber sassy u mama
I beet u haf de death

Boosie, git mama's 'suader, no boy
tak dem britches oft, I wont u ass

A TRUE FRIEND

Darkness, a place of comfort for me.
There are no little people on street
corners begging bread. There are no
news reports about death, dying, and
war. There are no preachers and
politicians talking about heaven, hell,
and tax increase.
Ah! Cover me and allow me to live a little,
it is so peaceful to feel your touch, hear
your silent voice, and know you are my
protector. You are great! When I am sane
you are there and when I drift off into
the world of insanity you are there.
I remember so well when you were my enemy
and I feared you more than death. You
came along in the late, late evening,
separated me from play, and hurled me into
blackness. Moments later I became
older and my innocence was gone forever.
You became my friend and I shared the deepest
of my secrets with you. Now you are a voyeur.
What the hell...you can keep a secret.

March 1986

IT'S COLD

Spring sunshine
Wind blows
Flowers dressed
Sunday's best
Birds fly
Singing songs
Vision of freedom
Use my face
It's a shit bowl
Join the crowd
Web feet
Three people shot
One is insane
Another in love
The other confused
They are all dead
A woman sold her color tv
Roasted her baby
Times are hard
Mommy died
I'm cold

I CAN READ

The old man stood before the people and spoke:
Now I am free to travel unknown roads and
decide which way I will go
By no means is my life perfect
but I am in control

I can read yesterday's history
interpret it for today's survival
and tomorrow's possibilities:
that is freedom

Crippled by parochial interest and limited
opportunity, the old man
dropped into a squeaky rocking chair
on his front porch and his mind
went back into reverse

July 1987

AMAZING GRACE

The old lady rolled out of bed
pain in every joint of her body
even her mind was in pain

Years of hard work and
rich night life had taken
their toll

She wobbled over to her
rocking chair by the
window

Looking out she began
to rock and hum, amazing
grace how sweet the sound

It was sunset
glowing orange
snowcapped mountain
transparent red to
her tired old eyes

Suddenly she stopped
humming and her fey
mind began to travel

Her past came over the screen
of her mind and
she wept

Then came a smile
over her prune face
the pain disappeared

August 1987

GEORGE-THÉRÈSE DICKENSON

George-Thérèse Dickenson is the author of *Striations*, 1976 (Good Gay Poets), and *Transducing*, 1985 (Segue). She was the founder and has been the director for the last ten years of Incision Arts. She has been editor of *Black Rose: A Journal of Anarchist Theory*, *Assassin*, and *Incisions: Prison Ward Poetry*.

from

THE INTERPRETER OF DREAMS

for José Antonio Martinez

I decided,
For example. Implore, oh God,
Adapted for film for fine
Measure for sight and other
Human senses and sensual
Promise and protean beauty
Become, oh Lord, in the
Light hours of the island
With its rocks and coral
Hills and haunted humps
Of earth bristling
And cactus and bulging
From a small waist to another
Set of promontories from which
The explorer sees all things
The good and the untamed
Things called up in your
Voice, born of your syntax,
And in your diction and
Melodious with grammar made
Of the moment for the street
On which you hold me or
Through which we move
Looking hand in hand
Watched and greeted and
Called all manner of things
Of beauty and couples of strong
Grace and warrior blood.
Popi, pops, pa, to my
Mothering hands on your dark
Forehead or rubbing oils in
Your thick black hair
In which spirits move and

Create pain and glory in the
Human mind that looks and
Finds and sees and becomes
Part of that which he always managed
To avoid. The streets stare. The
Stones newly placed for a
Gentry newly engaged to the
Neighborhood of stoops and stairs
And laundry hung from wires
Or needles piercing arms
In the sign of the cross in
The night forearm blood stains
The cloth tied and dropped
On the table with the letters to mail
And words on paper and works
On pages and sealed in boots
So I will not find the source
In the spring from stone
Which cries to be a cutting
Edge on your arm in the form
Of a cross borne by one who
Gives and loves and keeps
For himself in the middle of
Clothes and fights and men
And women and phone calls
Across the Mason-Dixon Line
With accents and accented ways
Of bearing the signs of one's
Birth with courts and tennis
Courts and fathers who come
And go and camps and
Counting baskets to the block
On which you are known and I
As yours no one will lift
A voice or finger to knowing
In knowledge of course I
Would have us people who work

No matter after he could do it
Again thrown for a loop. About
His speed, but kind of sick
Looking from a weed-grown
Trail or trail where no thing
Grows or trial Monday for
Which you've done nothing right.
I had an answer ready in
A tone to tilt the conversation
Or guarantee loss. I wanted
Him to come. There was a
Small port, a tiny, tight hole
A place to go, a refuge, a
Punk with arms of gold, a spot
Of welcome, a tiny hole for you.
A cove or cavern or
In a place to be of the place
Of birth yet of more of
Your self through rivers
And glens and streets and
Cities becoming villages because
You make them small and big
Or any thing else you want in
The dark night with dulled eyes
And sly ways and lies laying
Until daybreak awake to
The inner workings of the human mind
Made and making from her own responses
With exactitude and available
For distraction the internal
Telling too, I do not know.
Now listen I was overcome
I changed I am imagining
A changing self when we say
Or do we come I am listening
And talking to a soul inside
A structure to direct exposure

Or discreet experience or will intact
And scenes sounding like
Questions asked and avoided
Statements transmuted into
Long winding divergence in
Which we stand and over cliffs
From which we wave or walk
Together amid crags and cactus
And shells breaking in crashing
Tides the name you call
Me a life still writing itself
In words and inner logic
And aspected experience and
Aspects of every day and
Days do come and days leave
Behind days do well here days
Do in and do so of she was in
Days past and present and
To come with him she speaks
A primer or primary writing
His words—wet as a woman with
Confluence and transferring
Nature to call a thing one's
Own and make it conscious and
I will make myself
Conscious of my own self through
Conscious struggle and abstract
Thought in which he becomes
My sight or I him or his
Seeing into the life of the
Azure sky with deep-toned rocks
And caves hung with stalagtites
And false gold burning palms
And bloodstone pulling the pain
Out when placed just so I
Walked in him to see a man
Parsing the world and parting

Thighs and rearing and bucking
Begging for bounty in a heritage
To call his own I saw it coming
And asked for more.

And I told all the words and
Swords passed through who
Was with and will to those in
Time and of places
All his men had traveled
And women had built
And built lands and caverns
And cities called up with words
In active thought peering
Answered, I know or I will
Or I do with fire and through
Stones and stars, staring he came to me this
Day to say and save
Writing words to pierce the page
In consort and with consent
I call him up, here to the day
As it breaks over each portion
In a language created
For the occasion to live and die
So words come through the
Scene painted over like a sky
Appearing to be a man hoeing
A field under a big sky his
Wife calling him home over
Bold fields or fallow earth
Or in a dearth of fruit and
Time of plenty paid to lay low
So he did.

I think in the language, and I
Trained in work to be done for others.
He holds it. A piece of writing I

Do not think to do and write
Of a piece thinking and in thought and in many jointed
Senses as if there were no main
Thing but what we live
In writing words, speak.

I think he does. He does not.
Did the lackey lower the liveried
Flame to the goatherd's bell?
Does the triumph mark a master?
In a pool a playgirl extends
And tends toward the sun.
A fun thing to be a way of say
I come and craft is hearth for
Passage in creaky wheels
Shuffling along a proscribed course
A clinking curse, a camera, a care.

The sun comes in gradually
Through the trees and slips out again
Where I lay or lie alone.

The rat plays gin. The fire is
Bread to salt of soul, the naughty
Girl wants a goal, the sultry
Kid is in a jam, bleating and braying
From the widow's perch.
Sun lunges in. Clouds race.
A meadow lays on its side.
The guy can't help himself.

The island remains an island.
Sending tendrils under the ocean
But never connecting
A place for all manner of possible things,
A gulch where no one knows
Or sees so one can be what one

Is at the moment one says
It is today and I am here and I feel
Thus and therefore I do this or go
Connected to the mainland.
Relative to the island off by itself
In a far corner of the sea where I
Drink and toast the dawn or moon.

This is an explorer speaking. This
Is someone talking to oneself.
This is Barney and this is Jerry
And this is Jimmy turning yellow
At the end for a reason. This
Is not an example.

The boys are talking. Someone is
Talking in someone else's language
And telling stories and throwing stones
And climbing walls
Photographing from the windows
That wind back to pasts with
Many children and many junkie
Uncles and crying tropical breezes
Locked behind steaming or frosted
Glass in small rooms where his
Friend's aunt kept her children
A long time ago over again the shutter
Snaps on a car driven three blocks to
High school the kid parks
and exits and his mother waits
Behind windows calling on the saints
Or an older sister cares for the children
Left behind trying to forget.

Somewhere in the Bronx or somewhere
In Brooklyn or somewhere a big

Brother is offering his younger brother
A ride in a car to show him how good
The world can be. This is a word
Or a world of good which are of and even to
Be made and are made and
Given choices to make if we are the
Art of the twentieth century in God
In finite space and with a limited
Number of presents or present
Situations or possibilities present
Themselves in each passage or
Each passing moment of which a life
Can or cannot be made or lost in a
Choice to hold a gun for a friend
To pull a trigger to tell a story
To try your hand to hold court to curry
A favor to have a friend's back
Which means you are
A man among men
Encroaching a completely
Separate assertion a simple statement
A man unto himself a boy a
Brother. They built their houses
They paint the empty windows full
With curtains and plants and painting
Of glass over bricked-up windows in
Burned buildings. Various lines
Create a face on a page, a line moved
Turns the face away, a face looks out
A window and sees a street and
Watches a car drive uptown out of the
Blocks he's known the ball thrown
In a direct line through the basket
Gets the boy a scholarship gets the
Boy out of the block almost literate
The story goes mostly in language

He creates language I love
Approaching a lingering song
In a locked sky.

HECTOR ALGARÍN

Hector Algarín was born in Río Piedras, Puerto Rico, in 1952. He came to the United States with his family in 1956. Fluent in English, Spanish, Italian, and French, Hector has written a sizable body of poetry and prose, most of it as yet unpublished. He has had three children—two daughters and one son. He died in Saint Lucas Hospital in Newburgh, New York, and was buried on his birthday, August 22, 1987. He was thirty-five years old.

I THE PUPPET, YOU THE GOD

The stars in the sky remind me of your perfection,
the all-seeing eye. And I long to hear your voice,
informing me of what is sacred to me, of what is
supreme over me—you, the god of antiquity,
the lover of time, the father of the future.

You have tried many times to make me perfect, yet
I remain imperfect in your eyes because you really
have not tried hard enough. Through me you live and
experience my imperfections, like a puppeteer hidden
behind curtains, pulling strings that make me laugh,
walk, talk, and act very silly.

Then you rejoice because through my imperfections
you become the god and I the puppet.

You have made me in your image, but at times I wonder
if this is a joke, for when the wind is strongest I
spit at it in defiance of your powers. Then you, you
answer me by committing a blasphemy—you spit back
at your own image with your angry wind.

I don't know why you become angry. Maybe it's because
in my imperfections I am happy, human, and fallible
—and still in the muddy image of you.

CENTERFOLD

Oh, woman, mujer de mis esperanzas, out of one of my ribs you
were fashioned—perhaps that is why I cannot live without
you! When I look behind me you are always there...smiling.
Your smile but a cleverly devised facial movement that entices

me to sip the nectar of your lips, composed of
saliva: enzymes and starches. My adrenal-cortex responds to
your calling—intoxicating my thoughts—then I become
your prey and you are all I see. Without command yet
        commanded,

I lower my lips to your neck, a bundle of nerves, a passageway,
and in your ecstasy you exhale your germs upon my brow. Crazed,
I want all of you and bury my teeth in your mammary
glands—a mass of fat, a labyrinth of capillaries maintaining

the facade. Like a looter I become lawless and frantically commence
to grab grab grab all of you....Time elapses, I do
not know where it goes, but when I come to, I find my eyelids
fluttering against your silky skin, and my tongue exploring your

umbilical cord—and underneath, centimeters underneath, I
hear your entrails murmuring. I then become hungry and eat of
the Tree of Knowledge. I am no longer Adam. You are no
longer Eve. I seek your lifeline, you draw my blood—and

then, I look into your eyes and begin to admire your mind
one more time.

SANS FANTAISIE

Your realistic thinking has made a mockery of me,
not accepting my lily white lies that are the ideal
of your ideal self.

Like yesterday, they permeated the caucuses of your
mind, and I helped you be what you would never be.
Yes, you would never have been able to play hide-
and-seek with the truths and untruths if I had not
performed for you.

And, yes, I am sad and still cry when I knock
at the doors of your mind, and find your real self
standing there, garbled in a mesh of barbed wire,
and dressed in a thorazine-lined coat to keep you
from trembling. Your realness has become cold.

Yes, you cry for me, but your heart does not feel it.
Your tears are solid, they are clogging your thoughts.
With a straitjacket restraining you from harm, you
open your mouth to swallow your pineapple-coated thorazine.
The chilly season of winter has come
with my good-bye.

THE MIRROR

You send me this thought, which is the reflected thought
    every time our
Regards entwine in an amour-propre. Let not egoism be a
    product of your
Misconceived carnal plane fantasies. Underneath, skin and
    bones journey
Toward their inevitable fate: hole, decomposition, and oblivion.

I, who you see as you, am sad, because you...you will not
    truly
Know me, your reflection lost in the micro-seconds it'll take
    your eyes
To meet mine...

I, who you see staring back at you and you at *me*—afraid
    because when
You see your REALSELF transforming before your
    very eyes—you hurriedly
Blink!—so that again you may start staring back at *me*,
    who is you,
Your reflection and your past.

I, who you see as ancient, see your past and not your
    present, while
Our jailer, Father Time, mocks our illusion with the
    grammatical error
I see. I see instead of I saw the present become old before
    your very
Eyes, while mankind stares back at you as an emperor,
    a slave, a czar,
A serf, a bourgeois, a proletariat, a priest and a murderer!
    Then slyly
You granted your vanity a smile when you thought I was
    not looking.

I, who you see as your greatest enemy, am becoming myopic
    before your very
Eyes, while your principles quarrel with your limitations.
    Your ego gets
Jealous, he bites, then leaves the mark...there is nothing more.

A LIFER WHO IS A FRIEND OF MINE

(for Chuck Culhane)

The candle spends itself with an intense hope.
He lights another
after fashioning it from spent wax, to hope again.
He speaks with a drawl,
this friend of mine,
an exhausted drawl
as if it were travail to speak, a useless task
that rekindles memories of unwashed dishes
piling up with time.
Tap! Tap! Tap!
I hear as I cross his cell to get to mine
Tap! Tap! Tap!
Like a blacksmith at his anvil
he forges dreams
tears, and hopes—but all of wax!
Sometimes,
in a happy spell he *is* entitled to,
he opens wide his blue-sky eyes,
"All right...." he says in an exhausted drawl.
And then?
And then I cry wax tears
because I have a friend who needs them,
a lifer
who is a friend of mine.

7-85

66

O AZTEC, PRINCE, WHERE ARE YOU?

O Aztec, prince of the northwest hemisphere
Where are you who played with the stars

and

Deciphered them while the four winds
caressed your hair...

O Aztec, prince, where are you?
You who I wait for
to dry my tears of ignorance
that today get mixed up with the muddy waters
of the stream that yesterday quenched your thirst...

O Aztec, prince, where are you?
You who sacrificed the Mona Lisa to your God
to calm his furies, to placate his power

O Aztec, prince, where are you?
Read me the codices of the Sun calendar

and

Dry my tears of ignorance
that get mixed up with the bloody waters
of the stream that yesterday muddied your feet

O Aztec, prince, where are you

12-85

A SPECIAL BULLETIN

An appendage, a conglomerate blob of electrical inputs
supplying thoughts like an electrodialysis machine
plucks a corner of the naked and defenseless eye

watching. A marathon, a Three Mile Island with a
pothole to China, CBS in attendance while a bloated
fish — plutoniumed down — stares.

Tarzan hollers, selling lozenges to throatless mutes
while subliminally, at the speed of light, a naked
freak runs across the room

"Star Wars!" America cries; a terrorist sneezes;
the Soviets dare Geneva talks. An invisible and
patient hand stitches color tattoos on a collective mind

watching. A priest rapes a nun...not much blood
spilled today...a newsless day...
Beep, beep, beep, beep, beep, beep, this is a special bulletin:

An eye flinches in a sadistic stare.

PYRO-ORGASM

I have an obscene affinity for the red, white, blue,
and yellow fiery flames. They are doing an esoteric
dance on the Devil's breath, and calling out my name.
I have found my true vocation on Passover, stealing the preacher's
Holy Book, and in an abracadabra-ish ceremony,
I laid God's words to rest in a pyro of my own design.
Dance! Dance!
My senses screamed and my irises contracted in delight.
Sweat sluiced down my face. My heart banged at my chest door
as I watched the Devil's blood lick and caress the Holy Book
into a chalky white color.
Dance! Dance!
I have not known any prettier flames.
They danced and read to me, with an obscurantist's lick,
God's words with the Devil's blood!
Dance! Dance!
I came down from my orgasmic high,
and out of breath, wandered upstairs to fetch my sheepskin.
It certified me as a nuclear scientist
so that I might better dance the dance again.

6-85

A SUICIDE NOTE:

I've searched (and found!) in the hypothalamus region
of man's warmongering mind, the panacea. I left it
for you in the freezer, in the upper right-hand corner.
There it sits prettily, as a monument to my intellectual
greatness, cold and eerie-looking, and ready to proclaim
my name in a brouhaha of parental love. Yes! I *did*
become a member of the Academy of Science. And I received
from a friend (who had had his share of loud explosives)
some blood money from his conscience that recoiled in
spasms of cold shame. I was the elite, the chosen few,
the one who really understood you—your nature and your
safety. Do not fret. It sits in the freezer, patiently
waiting to gratify your most secret desire...
No, do not fret...

                    Dad

THE ANT FARM

The day comes and goes, and the work is always there
for one body to take the place of another:
Out they come like ridges over the land mass
to collect their daily crumbs of whatever, to bring

To their Queen in the hole by the land where tomorrow
they will die. Because it is their job to supply their
mother and brothers and tomorrows...and their
feelers are twitching and searching for their enemy and

Friend in a day when time and harmony is the only
friend they have and will always work for. Many little
ones working for their mother and brothers and tomorrows,
and slowly they near the ledge of their destiny

And down they go to give a chance to another.

A PRISONER'S SONG

Bucephalus' reins, buried deep near a dream,
are attached to tomorrows that are smeared by today
Despair nearly trembles while the hopes shy away
and the seeds of old memories
dance and laugh at their wake

       Recalling a day when the voice was not heard,
       only vibes, surrounding, palpable,
       obscuring the green face of freedom;
       On piggyback, an exhausted raffler
       multiplied oubliettes with Napier's bones
       to add souls forgotten by a broken rule,
       and a blind lady in dregs weighed
       the unweighable: Freedom

Bucephalus' eyes stare intently: A dream far away;
A lover's pudendum run amok in his mane;
Cockaigne dressed in honey. Knitting hands never wave
The phantom illusions
help the pain go astray

       Perceiving the autumn leaves knitting time,
       bringing nearer a laminated dream,
       holding it fast—a product of abnormality—
       a blind man out of his element,
       the awaited site. Violets in a cemetery;
       a CARE package to Hell

Bucephalus' whinny on a crutch falls halfway
and the nine Gran Señores whose ears are spaded
hear no echo. The cry dies in vain
and the action of speaking
chips the steel that maims

A strained vocal cord flagellated
by an insomniac desire to be heard,
calling out in vain—
many names—
and acknowledged
by a coagulation of shame

Bucephalus' body shackled raw to a gate
Bucephalus' heart...
Bucephalus' soul...
The time keeps passing
and his mane becomes snow.

12-85

JANINE POMMY VEGA

Janine Pommy Vega is the author of *Poems to Fernando*, 1968 (City Lights); *Journal of a Hermit*, 1974 (Cherry Valley Editions); *Morning Passage*, 1976 (Telephone Books); *Here at the Door*, 1978 (Zone Press); *Journal of a Hermit &*, 1979 (Cherry Valley Editions); *The Bard Owl*, 1980 (Kulchur Press); *Apex of the Earth's Way*, 1984 (White Pine Press). Two new books will be coming out in 1988: *Aves Salvajes del Corazón* (Wild Birds of the Heart) from Las Lluvias Press in Lima, Peru and *Drunk on a Glacier, Talking to Flies* from Tooth of Time Books in New Mexico. Ms. Vega lives in Bearsville, New York, and works in New York State Poets in the Schools in New York City and upstate New York. She was co-founder of the Sing Sing Poetry Workshop and has been its co-director for the past four years.

LURIGANCHO

A solitary air blows over the cerro
the sun, disguised in the white
soup of Lima, is vaguely waving

Guards with official whistles
harry the listener
calling each other through corridors
they shriek and answer
shriek and answer
barking dogs at midnight
in a little town—
the visits are over

Brick walls, broken windows
inmates in brightly colored shirts
are waving
the only flower in the grainy air
the only color

Holes are broken through brick walls
into cubicles
to search outsiders
the left arms of women tattooed with
numbers
the personal shakedown
leaving, we file through again
for the last touch, across the crotch,
to prove we are women

Outside the walls, machine guns strut
through abandoned market days
leering into the hurried business
of thousands of women
struggling into lines for the buses

exchanging news and embraces
to last the week
the men at the windows are waving
waving

Saludos, hermanos
where we know each other
there are no walls
no twisted dreams of day after day
but a clear wind over the Andes
the gentle touch of garúa moistening
hands and hair

Ciao, South American continent
the murders in your face
are less disguised than where I live—
one sees who to hate
to the north the civilized killers,
corporate fists, the ones in power
have no human face at all.
They have no face.

*Lurigancho, a men's prison outside
Lima, Peru, September, 1982*

AMERICAN ARTISTS

My friends and I sat on the
picnic table
we talked about how the world was
how we wanted it to be
the table was slanted
we ate our lunch
a cold air running through our fingers

who knows about the farms inside
the ones we carry around
— if the crops are gathered
or the well is dry
or the roots
wrenched out of the earth?
we sat together and ate our lunch

half revealed in the gray light
were the stones of ourselves, our bones
and molars, none of us were fat
nor clearly defined
lines wavered about the chin as the roads
composed themselves
and the landscapes settled

an element of fear sat in the scarred
photographs, the torn posters
and revelatory dreams
a complicity of misery in the gnarled
hands of sharecroppers, migrant workers
exiles born out of a country
no one saw any more

then, like a wind buried in the tree line
that comes singing over the heads
of the farmers a forgotten tune
someone laughed
we all laughed
we jumped up and down on the table
the farms followed us home.

Willow, NY, October 1985

SING SING CHRISTMAS

(for Julian)

To whom shall I describe
my happiness?
Every last bit of minutiae fallen into place
until the stage
swept clean at last
stands witness to the fabulous work in progress
a steady stream of applause coming
from the universe
the constellations joined in a 3-D cup
'Embriagadora felicidad' says Pablo
and I believe him
moments like these
when the cells are coated with sweat
and tears and laughter
of love, aimed at the I
who is not I
the one who remains standing when I
have died, the one who waits
smiling
while I look for my shoelace behind
the bureau, or I'm doing something else
and don't look up.

Sing Sing, NY, December 18, 1985

THE WALK

A woman, twisted at the edge of her seat,
walks into the woods
walks blindly, she intends to scream
she intends to walk to the old friend, the
hickory tree at the top of the road,
and fling her arms around him, and pound
the snow at his feet.

Instead, she walks a little farther.
She doesn't want the light across the meadow
in on her screams; the family in there, blanking
out the sound during commercials, alerted suddenly
to the wild dreams of trees.
She continues climbing, past the maple tree of a hundred
walks, her feet striding purposefully
into the dark.

The stars come suddenly to her, decorating
the arms of the forest—Orion, Sirius, Pleiades,
Hyades, Auriga, Perseus, and Algol the demon star
thrust away from him
Due north Polaris over the brow of the hill
And she doesn't want to build another bookshelf
She doesn't want to pocket this away,
to squirrel it in some quiet corner where she will
never find it again.

She reaches the stream. It is the only darkness
in the forest, and the only time she takes out
her flashlight. Where she was stepping was indeed
a rock. What she reached for was the water.
Her hands are warm. It is an old pact
between her and the beech trees rustling on the path.
Her war is with herself, herself and containment

Not against the footsteps of a path, or the sensible
way out, but against the ironing out of wildness,
her own wildness.

Her heart is stirred as a creature under the trees
looking up at lights. No wind, the tears roll down
her face. She is safe in her love for the stars,
the water, her commitment to beauty.
Is it beauty, really? Does it matter?
She doesn't build shelves, nor bookcases, with
every book a brick one keeps for safety hidden
in the corner. Her love turns a corner,
it dips over the rise in the hill, and whoops down
the other side. Perhaps her books will be kisses,
wet leaves under the snow that show up dark
on a moonless night.

Perhaps she will never reach Jerusalem on a camel,
or see the Southern Cross again. The north woods
is where she happens to be, divining the branches before
they hit her face. Perhaps she will never build
a bookcase. Perhaps she doesn't have to.

Willow, NY, January 1986

LITTLE GHOST IN THE STATION

(for Richard Manuel)

Looking through the window down the track
to the north, she peeled a piece of plastic
from the pane
the birds would have a hard time of it
tonight, the frozen wind, the waves
looping and crashing on the rocks,
especially the migratory ones,
the white-throated sparrow who had just
appeared in the courtyard yesterday
and sung his heart out

The plastic scraping rose in the draft
from the track below
and she thought of her mother
her mother who thought of birds
on the fiercest mornings, and threw
them bread with bacon drippings,
The plastic fluttered up again,
a tiny dybbuk in the window corner,
a tiny message from her mother,
a voice in the phone from far away

She worried about the birds, too
especially that one, God's flute player
who gave her spring at the fire escape
when she whistled and he answered
the same four notes he sang in the Catskill
summers when she reached a peak
"Poor John Is Dead," he sang
and now it was winter, quiet at the window,
and she did not need a cigarette
she needed to weep.

Ossining, NY, February 1986

MR. PLANT, A PORTRAIT

A goat jumps over a pile of leaves,
a green plant, to be specific,
and it's Tuesday
he jumps through the door wearing
sneakers, humming to himself

It's a large square room we have
for the workshop, outside are
the armed guards
on the windows, bars
and in this room a freedom that
like some champagnes
doesn't travel

Mr. Plant's in a chipper mood
slinging around *damp cap*
two sounds he likes, until he
fits them perfectly into the picture
of a wall, a damp wall, and an army
marching foolishly down the track

on that blue/red star he calls
home his laugh is easy
his biggest jokes reserved for
himself, the human bean, the silliest
of God's creatures

the sun goes down over the Palisades
and over the river brilliant bands
of gold serenade the eye
and from the blue/red star the plant
looks out the window.

Sing Sing, NY, April 1986

OMAR AND THE DRAGON

Over the charred remains of
a ruffled skirt
is Omar
deeply in love
kissing her elbow, her wrist, her hand,
his head intent over her wristwatch
on the divan; official hankies
drape themselves from the windows

O to be young again! he cried
to the seraphs in the alcove
with my own pawn shop!
She stirred languorously
in maroon felt grandmother slippers
dreaming of possible exits
into Chinatown, the portholes of her eyes
into dragon vessels

Chinese junks sailed stately
into the drawing room
where port wine and moustaches glimmered
in the light from the harbor

Upside down now Omar found her
anchored to her backbone
like a figurehead
almost Christlike on the yardarm
waiting
for him to push her off the edge
of the sofa, into the sea.

Sing Sing, NY, March 1987

THE FLOOD

Archangel Mary falls into the water
killing the bridges, the Tappan Zee and
railroad trestles. Her backside against
the pier, they promenade
across her, River Edge to Harlem,
and time runs out

Archangel Mary, dressed as a chorus girl
waits by Big·Ben in the harbor
It's not midnight yet, she stands
in the cascades covering her face,
kicks out from the deluge in Paris
and dreams in bed

He watches her through the bars
and thinks she's trapped
She is sleeping
flood waters rise
She is safe and smiling
caught in a dream of sunlight
shining on the coins around her face

Out of the Bedouin desert her ankle
steps into a taxi in London
Someone offers her a ring, the coins
hide her face
She is safe and smiling, playing the piano
in a solemn moment, water pours through
her window to the street

He has come down from the rooftop
in a suit of chimneys
In her private ocean Archangel Mary
watches him sail by the quay
She lights a candle in the mirror
She likes his face.

Sing Sing, NY, May 1987

HUMAN PRAYER

Sing Sing entrance
stands over the shoreline
of the Hudson River

to the left
behind barbed wire topped wall
is a ball field
someone hits a triple as the sun
goes down

to the right
sprawled along the river
is lover's lane, a kid
peels out in a blue car,
the squeal of tires

and one side is inside
and one side is outside
the same plane passing through
the same sky over both

inside, walking out
through stone corridors
I rub a little lipstick on the wall.

Sing Sing, NY, June 1985

RETURN TO SENDER/ INMATE IS DEAD

for Hector Algarín

Dear Hector:
this is how your letter came back
and the job does not get easier
Our casualties behind the wall are buried
with numbers instead of names,
numbers that have nothing to do with birthdays,
dreams, or completed works:
What are the odds we can make
a dent in the system?

I want everyone in this country
to stop that train, says Brian Wilson,
Viet Nam vet peace activist
I'm driving down Interstate 90, holding
your letter in my lap while he lays on
the tracks. And gone! His legs are gone!
Mowed down by munitions train bound with bombs
for Nicaragua: What are the odds we dent in
a cast-iron system?

I'm pulling out every Sing Sing folder
looking for you—your poems, your letters,
your voice on the Christmas tape
over and over
Jigsaw pieces. The person I know caught
in glimpses, much like the mirror you
spoke into at the Christmas reading

In a room with too many lights on
a paper clip dropped in a stone bowl
makes three syllables—a tiny sound—
and I know the mortality I carry
in my breastbone, the tilt of my shoulders
The river, swollen with rain, is roaring

RETURN TO RETURNER/ INMATE IS NOT DEAD

Inmate is not inmate.
Bucephalos whinnies into starry space.
The blood under the bridge *is* the bridge.
The miracle is a green face of freedom:
No them. Just all of us.

Willow, NY, September 1987

CHUCK CULHANE

I'm 42 years old (August 1987) and have been in prison for nearly 21 years straight. I'm a survivor in the sense that the time hasn't warped me. One motto I had a few years ago was "Dented but not daunted!" and I feel that's a valid self-perception. To grow in any environment is seldom a matter of accident; but in addition to making some correct choices, I've had the great good fortune of having a wonderful family and of meeting good friends along the road. Most recently I married a fine woman and fellow abolitionist, Anne Watkins, and I feel blessed in many ways. Years ago my mother cautioned me to count my blessings, and sometimes it gets to the point where I don't have enough fingers to do that and find myself just raising and opening my hands to the sky, giving and receiving. I think a decent poem does that, or attempts to: to give back some of what is received. It's an honor to be in the same book with real writers and poets, Janine, Jack, Hank, Hector, Jimmy, and George-Thérèse. I salute them, and hope together we can dispel some of the myths and stereotyped images about life, thought, and feeling behind the walls.

SPRING CLEANING

The softy in me leaves bread for the mice
the price is to clean up the shit
now and then.

Like yesterday, a torn white towel
into the bucket with a soapball,
the hot gray water swirling
forms a heart in the sea of suds.

Two bits whirl together at the center,
their shapes distinctive:
I see a tadpole, a tree,
equidistant like yin and yang
merging and reemerging
in an exotic water dance.

Where now aquatic creatures?
There! The mermaid!
And there! Icarus
descending in a parachute.
She swims under. And, oh, he joins her.

Attica, 1983

AFTER ALMOST TWENTY YEARS

(for Judge Rose Bird)

This is getting difficult.

Perhaps there's another formula
    for happiness and contentment
    I haven't explored or exhausted yet.

But I talk to birds.
I have to put in my partial plates tho
w/tip of index finger fanning wet lips

        do it!

      the sound near-identical
      which amazes me.

Recently the birds woke me up
    with their clamorous love
      wings beating around the bars and glass
        in animated flight
jailbirds in the rush of lusty spring.

I was barely awake, grumbling at my broken sleep
then somehow drawn out
    into the quiet light
    sitting on the side of my bed.

And there they were
        two of em
          beaking it up!
Oh! I could've fallen into curled glee
    wound with the spring's redemption.
And the nest already built
    under the highest beam in the block.

Sing Sing, 1984

IN THE VISITING ROOM

My sister Kathy went to the bathroom
and I couldn't help but hear the couple arguing.

He with false pride, counting her failings
She, w/lost hope, defending her sacrifices.
He had no ear for her love it seemed
or it was an ear so low
in that place where prison
can cut men
with cold silence and anger
and to fight back is right and ok, man
but not with the one who loves you.

She turned to the river.
I knew her eyes were glistening.
And I looked out the big window
And felt like crying.

When my sister returned
I saw they started to make up.
Such a handsome couple.
They must've been so close once.

Sing Sing, 1986

UNTITLED

In the morning God sticks a yellow card
in His main machine.

All over the city radios get going
people pop up from their pillows
and start running around.

Refrigerators and stoves smile at each other
bathroom doors and elevators argue
cars and streetlights holler at cobblestones
subways and escalators sing love songs
factories goof on office buildings
bridges complain to the rivers
schools and churches huddle in quiet conspiracies
police stations and hospitals start crying
parks and penny arcades open their green arms
restaurants and theaters wave to buses and taxis
and God thinks: Tomorrow I'll try blue.

Attica, 1981

SPARSER

(for Whaylen)

This spartan prayer for peace
amidst the carnage and carnival
    of autumn:

A spear of praise in the river
thin light on the water
a small sailboat bobbing into it:

I saw this today
stopping on the iron stairs
through the sere trees
sparser in leafgrowth.

What joy the boatfolk must've known
slowtumbling downriver
towed by another twilight
with its daily toll of spills
long stretches of stolid passages
and there, a phosphorescent spot
    of heaven's grace
a narrow island of light.

Oh to have seen their faces
and the rapt salute of the spars
as the frail assemblage
breaks for a safe harbor.

Sing Sing, 1986

BUSY PRISONER

(for Thelma)

After lunch, which he didn't eat
he stacked the folders, which he didn't carry
to take to the office where he didn't go.

But he left the cell
with a painting under his arm
and a cigar stuck in his mouth
after putting the laces in his boots
        through the top loops
        (a job he'd postponed for two months).

After leaving the cell
he went back in and out four times
        for whatever he kept forgetting
        or remembering
        and eventually made it to the yard
        with its slim carpet of snow.

There were two prisoners and two guards
huddled in the light cold near a blue picnic table.
"Reinforcements are here!" he exclaimed cheerfully
then walked around the yard once
and started jogging
fast, slow, backwards, sideways, skipping, sprinting
even thought about doing a cartwheel.

Then off to the side where the weights are
an indented space
bordered by the old river and retired death house.
He slumped against a fence, coughing
then trudged back up the hill to call his friend
        down in Georgia.

Sing Sing, 1985

A MEDITATION ON A MAX ERNST DRAWING

Max, what are you up to
with this guy knocked out by fire?
Stunned on a stone floor
in a vaunted chamber of desire.

Evidently he is sapped, burnt out
by this plump Athena with great tits
and supple revenge.

He is dead, no question.
Six candles burn in memory town
and he, hot at both ends—
attaway to go!

Sing Sing, 1986

AFTER CATULLUS

Did you see the wedding march winding
without bells? The belly of the entire city
is calling to the houses of neglect.
Today even cold whores dance, fuck our failings,
the only sordid flesh is in the past.

Do you not believe me? cried Pollion's
father. With your silent talents
inscribe these bright words:
Into this world of lepers we come,
cut among factions,
strange, with 11 names and 300 hopes.

These words our neglected houses
give back to us,
not boxed in like our own whimperings,
or rumors of forgotten unions,
but *names* under the sun...

Sing Sing, 1985

DAMP CAP

I rummage through piles of paper
trying to pull a poem out of the woods.
I read all the jumbled imagery and sounds
trying to find a symmetry
and all I come up with are two words:
damp cap.

I like the sound, the feel
a firm fit
like congealing glue in the brainpan
or rain crowning a warm wall.

Said fast it sounds like a dumb German march:
dampcap! dampcap!
Said slow the flutter of giant moth wings:
damp   cap   damp cap.

Sing Sing, 1985

AUTUMN YARD

I sit bundled in the peaceful sun.

To my right, a slip of colored sail
      goes downriver
      behind the old death house.

Two prisoners circle a dirt path
      bordering a green field
      double-fenced and walled
      with liberal layers of barbed wire.

Buck, a Lifer, works on the bars
      doing chins and dips
      building his house trim and strong
      against the long years.

George, hands scrunched in wordless pockets
      walks with recent loss
      of his young brother.
We nod hello, and faded pennants
      snap in the wind along the fencetop.

                    Sing Sing, 1985

FIRST DAY OF HANUKKAH

Old Doc, my neighbor
in his dark wrinkled prison clothes
in the dim tier-light of evening
put out his cell light
put on an electric blue yarmulke
over wild shocks of white hair.

Inseparable from weighty congested traffic
of bodies each with its own language
mumbling along the edges of concrete confusion
bracketed by cries of steel & silent histories
moving through daunting time, somber, calm
guilt and expiation emblazoned along neon walls
as clear as unseen galaxies, as uncertain.

Amidst the bustle & the boredom
of maximum security life
he lit three candles on the bars
& sat on the end of his bed w/prayerbook.
He prayed in the small light
in his sixty-ninth year
neither murderer nor holy man
just a bit of bone & spirit
remembering the song beyond the ruins.

Sing Sing, 1986

OF COLD PLACES

for Anne Watkins

I used to keep a list of foreign prisons:
Lubyanka in Moscow, Portolova in Spain,
California's Terminal Island,
exotic names of cold places.

And I thought: one day I'll make a poem
listing all the names
and conjure from their histories
hard memories
of humans among stone.

I'm older now, the lists grow
the edges of paper curl up, turn brown.
The names still cry out
without voice
without ear to hear them
and I can't remember what it was
I was supposed to do
except live nearer the fire.

Sing Sing, 1984

FOR HECTOR ALGARÍN

There was a tiger in that small body
with wide and hungry wanderings
and curious soul
rolling speeches from history
intoxicated son
beating the drum of bewildered facts
bivouacking with fleeting knowledge
no buoys for your lost ships
just soundings of exotic clouds and rocks
flesh-echoes rubbing the hard truth.

How did you know these things?
what the horse felt
in his platonic and noble stead,
you said these beasts are our legacy
the eternal war for the little
left at the core of ourselves
what we call so many names
learning past the masks
shaped with rain
cleaning our murky hopes
gone back into the wax
for a little more use
measuring the sense of our follies
and the jaundiced eye we save
for the terrible icons
we break with love and helplessly
try to put back together
neither what was nor what is
but mere semblance of dreams
grappling in the dust
for the maps
with their awesome coordinates.

Finger to the heart the only road we know
the rest is guessing and then we die
but you so young, in your flowering.
Adios, hermano, blood poet with the mirror.

Sing Sing, 1987

*Neither in the hearts of men nor in the manners of society will
there be a lasting peace until we outlaw death.*
                                        —Albert Camus

LAST CHRISTMAS FOR DEATH ROW·

I

In the Pacific a Polish tanker goes down,
All hands are lost, are drowned.
In Nicaragua the city of Managua weeps rivers
And the salt of dreaming children fills the Caribbean.
In Hanoi, presents from the Pentagon whistle from the sky
Piling corpse-ash and despair before the door of the world.
In Missouri, old Harry's giving up the ghost—
So goes the news of Christmas at 6 p.m.
But, who's to say that the sea is not our home?
That life is not eternal?
That a determined people are not protected?
That Hiroshima is not endless forgiveness?
Or that the smiles and dreams of children
Cannot redeem this Christmas?
Not I.

Out there beyond this prison a vision goes on
That we in here and the self within the we
Seem not to be a part of
Though we are.
We too
Walk in the light and shadows of days and nights,
Have smiles and tears, dreams and nightmares,
Are unique equal fragments in a greater dream—
We too need to share in tomorrow.

In here 1400 men dwell in the silence of their cells,
Alone.
Thinking thoughts of what and when and why,
Having feelings about who and where and how,

105

Just like people everywhere.
Even closer to it in here sometimes,
For what are prisons but social metaphors
That say we're all imprisoned in unreal ways.
And what are walls and bars but physical symbols
That those out there impose on those in here.
In here the symbols are visible and real,
They are steel and concrete.
It's not difficult to see
A small cage holding racial antipathy,
A gun-tower structured along poverty lines,
Or a sexist angle on a thirty-foot wall—
Not difficult to see at all if you care to look.
Look, prisons are not in tomorrow,
They're wrong, and the recognition of a wrong means nothing
Until it becomes the need to amend it.
To ignore or fear what is known to be wrong
Is to give substance to its false existence.
To face it and transform it is the only real choice
For everyone, everyone
In structured steel or mental form
Is imprisoned till everyone is free.

II

Tonight I hesitate to celebrate.
The Christmas obscured in department stores
Has little to do with Christ.
Yet there's always cause for celebration,
Every moment is worthy of praise—Christ said that.
Tonight I indulge my death row appetite,
Write as I feel, and say that despite all the problems in life
It's a good journey.
Tonight I give praise to my cell,
It's my home in standard Bethlehem, good steel.
My lightbulb is at least a star.
Tonight I give praise to Joseph, my brother,

To Mary, my sister,
To my mother and father, the Oneness,
Keepers of the Keys, arbiters of time and space
Wherein I travel.
I give praise to the passing of death row,
Last Christmas for the electric chair—
It was nothing but a mistake, the mystique of death is gone.
600 lives later, I give praise to the whitewashed room above,
Wherein sits a wooden lifeless tree of civilized insanity—
And it shall take no more life in New York.
Give praise to the demise of mindless and spiritless power,
Give praise to the death of legalized murder.

I give praise
To the enlightened though belated and ambivalent
U.S. Supreme Court decision in *Furman versus Georgia*,
To Anthony Amsterdam, Jack Himmelstein, Jack Greenberg,
To Douglas Lyons, to the NAACP Legal Defense Fund,
To all persons in the fight against death in this country,
To the day when Nigeria and South Africa stop the killing,
To the day when France stops chopping off heads,
To the day when Greece and Spain, Iraq and Iran stop the killing,
To the day when Russia and the Philippines outlaw firing squads,
To the day when the death penalty is universally abolished,
To the recognition of this as essential to human evolution,
To the great significance and sanctity of all life-forms.
I give praise to New York for almost electrocuting me.
I give praise to my wonderful family and their endless love.
I give praise to the courage and innocence of my friend Gary,
To Raheem, Bubba, and Fitz, brothers on the row.
I give praise to the wealth we found in this poor place.
I give praise to the knowledge that I am not bitter.
And lastly, I give praise and dedicate this poem to my friend Joan
With love and light at Christmas and always.

Green Haven, 1972